DROPS IN BLACK SAND

Sefa Noir

Andrea Johnson Books Publishing

Acknowledgements

For JS- In remembrance

For GM-Who inspired this dream

For AM- Whose support was immeasurable

For SN & MN-Whose Faith Sustained Me

For LC – Who Saw the beauty in the words

For DM - Who refused to let me give up

Kawo! Kabiosile Sango

Drops in Black Sand

© 2019 Sefa Noir. All rights reserved

Cover art designed by Andrea Johnson Books Publishing & Drexel McMillan, graphic artist.

No part of this book may be reproduced, stored in a retrieval system, or transmitted by any means without the written permission of the author.

First published by Andrea Johnson Books Publishing. 05/06/2019

6565 N. MacArthur Blvd, Suite 225 Dallas, TX. 75039 www.Ajbpublishing.com

This book is a work of fiction. Names, characters, places, and incidents are the product of the author's imagination or are used fictitiously. Any resemblance to actual events, locales, or persons, living or dead, is coincidental.

Because of the dynamic nature of the Internet, any web addresses or links contained in this book may have changed since publication and may no longer be valid. The views expressed in this work are solely those of the author and do not necessarily reflect the views of the publisher, and the publisher herby disclaims any responsibility for them.

ISBN: 978-0-578-45080-3

Table of Contents

The Surrender - 6
Will you Read Me? / My Black Man / When we met / Perfect Love / My saudade / What I Know / The Wonder of You / Sefa Noir-Dark Pleasure / Lost / That Day

The Completion – 39
The Attraction / All That I Am / His / If He Knew / I Want to Love You / The Soles of My Feet / Again / I am Bound / The Tidal Wave / Connected

The Submission – 70
Air and Earth / King / Know This / I Want to Know You / Be Free / Redeem Me / Imprinted on My Soul / My Scars / His Secret

The Recognition – 99
The Letter / Your Queen / Waiting / A Petition / My Love is Dying / For Love / Possession / 20 Years / Lifetime / Replenish Me / His Kingdom

Foreword

As a child of the late '60's I was raised in paradise… a paradise and I never knew it. A paradise of quiet, suburban bliss that I was ignorant of, where African Americans had achieved just enough but not too much to make the majority uncomfortable. I grew up in the era of Marvin Gaye playing on the radio of my mom's powder blue Chevy, and the birth of educational public television. My world was perfect – not because of wealth, as I am sure my parents will say there were days when we were only one or two paychecks from the poor house – our 2-bedroom apartment was full of family, yet food always made it to the table and new shoes on my feet. My mother made magic happen every Christmas, and favorite Saturdays were spent learning the hustle with my sister and dancing on my father's feet.

It was my heaven – I was surrounded by married aunts and uncles, the wisdom of loving grandparents, and the steadfastness of my parents love for one another no matter how trying each circumstance might be. Paradise began to fade, although I didn't always notice it – it crept up silently and discreetly like a thief in the night, it came at a time when it was still taboo to say you were gay or lesbian, and it was the un-written rule to date your own kind. I noticed the change when my uncle broke the color barrier, and brought home his very own blue-eyed beauty, and she became a part of our family. My mirror to the world changed, no more were the photos of Afro-puffs, and smooth dark "Ambi" skin, and my high school fears of not being "black enough" had transformed. My reality had begun to transcend, and it gave way to the college challenges of how you can assimilate, and the new image staring back was wearing weave and color contacts.

The invasion had begun, other races began to see the strength in our final asset. They wanted a piece of our resolute and dark mysterious love, they began taking over my heaven bit by bit; from the Nicole Brown-Simpsons, to the Kim Kardashians, they arrived in droves and the "James and Florida" images that once flooded my television gave way to the white-washed "Cliff and Claire" of the 80's. We were no longer those "people", we had become the prize to be obtained again and visions of strong black love began to fade in its midst, no more beautiful couples like Ozzie and Ruby or the young, defiant teachers on "Room 222".

All the while as the universe and my existence changed, there was always one absolute … My parents, whose example of love and dedication bore truth in living out the words that follow in these pages, and may all that read them see the strength of character in their being, and be inspired to have one day, and find a love like theirs…

Willie & Gladys

The Surrender

Will you read me?

Will You Read Me?

Beloved,

My words are not given so freely, carelessly, or unknowingly. There is true consideration for the message being communicated and the depth of the emotion behind it or missing from it, that I convey to you. When I write to you, I write for you, I write about you, I feel each word, and my pen becomes an extension of my touch.

I close my eyes and envision how you perceive, receive and hear my thoughts. I feverishly write each line with the hope of giving you a very small piece of myself verbally, literally, concretely, all of it inscribed to you in each text, poem, email, and brief message.

How desperately I want you to sense me through my language, and find intimacy with me in each word. Smart lines, clever humor, seductive sentences, and sharp quips to entice you is not who I am. I am wordy, poetic, verbose, and multi-syllabic. I am conversational, chatty, and self-proclaimed lecturer.

I am a writer, novelist, and speaker of my own truth-an amalgam of pages of un-ending paragraphs of compounded sentences, and edited grammar- all full of emotion, passion, anguish, energy, pain, dreams, darkness, masochism, obsession and love. Sentiments derived from literature, art, thesauri, dictionaries, encyclopedias, and foreign languages, history, and reference materials have created this unabridged library that exists in my head. All unforgotten lines from obscure authors, classic tales, bed-time stories, and sidewalk graffiti compiled into one immense Nordic Ode, a Shakespearean tragedy all my own.... I am stockpiling words.

Words to give, and convey to that one, who I am and where they place in my existence. Beloved, to me you are universal, expansive, un-matched, and limitless...your dominance transcends the confines of language as your power is revealed in the simple flex of your fingertips against my flesh, and it changes color.

Kings do not need to be reminded that royalty courses through their veins, and warriors never forget their weapons. You are my color, hue, brightness, depth and dimension, an artisan of strength on a palette of sadism.

Definitions often seek you for clarity, you are alchemy embodied... and walls crumble in your presence. You are the bricklayer who destroyed my foundation only to allow me to see yours. You found delight in my ruins because your intent was to rebuild me better than I was. You have left me starving and hungry but only wishing to be consumed. I thirst for your mark, opening myself to you only.... Will you read me????

My Black Man

My Black Man

Beloved,

I am craving that moment, that deep sensation from within... there is an artistic beauty when he "stiffens" in your presence... and his artistry is most profound because he is "My Black Man".

There is a depth within him you will not see in any other, as his melanin skin provides the perfect shading - it is deep, rich and mystical just as the culture he is born from. The veins in his member pop with knowledge and purpose, I am entranced when his nature begins to rise.

All I can think of is how much I need to feel him, absorb his pulse with every thrust, to feel him deeply with each push. "My Black Man" is real, not an ethnic fetish to be chased - he is palpable, transcendent ... defined only by the chemistry that seeps gently from his skin.

He is worthy to be seen, a man among men, to be tasted with all the senses, not merely to be touched. There is energy in his orgasm that doesn't exist in another. Women seek him out to satisfy their craving, they want to be infused with "My Black Man's" vibe, they recognize the healing in his sexuality.

Not his stamina or his member, but simply his composition deem all others inferior. His singular design drips from his pores when he sweats - he brings color to every racial palette; the strength of his character make his dominance oh so delicious.

Women of every nation line up for just one drop of "My Black Mans'" fluid, they need his power deep from within his orgasm, it radiates and draws them in. Genetically engineered for a myelinated woman's womb. Strong in its make-up - intended to replenish "his beloved earth".

There is foundation in his very semen, as he enters, we become the edge of the universe - the beginning of all time. He sees me as I am, naked and vulnerable. Simplicity in shades of black and white - "My Black Man" can sense my calmness-the peace within me because in that moment, I am real and waiting only for him.

When we met

When We Met

Beloved,

When we first met, I could immediately tell by the tone in your voice, the swagger in your step, and the sharpness of demeanor, that I could neither be or would be the great love of your life.

I had sincerely hoped that instead your wounds would soften, and your heart would begin to beat again, and that one day you would come to revel in the knowledge that you had met someone that loved you enough to want you to become "their great love"

That someone trusted enough in the truth and promise of your character to allow you into their heart, mind, body, and soul, believing that it might reignite within you even if only the smallest flames of passion again.

As the scent, you wear daily mixes with your masculinity and it becomes you, I close my eyes to imagine you. It brings you forever closer yet at a distance always. There is this ache that exists deep in my core, for you are my Saudade... that pain that I delight in and that sickness I long to enjoy again.

When we first met ... I knew I needed to be yours.

Perfect Love

Perfect Love

Beloved,

My love is not perfect ... it is loud and brash and stands out boldly among the crowd screaming for you.

My love is not perfect .... many days my love is dark and twisted...obsessive and needy. It begs to be owned by you.

My love is not perfect ....it is weak and sensitive and hungry for your attention; it writes to you at 3am desperate for a reply.

My love is not perfect...it is quiet and tearful and fears that you may be lost from me; it longs to hear the words you are mine.

My love is not perfect... but it lives and breathes for the mere thought of you, it is committed and giving, breathless in your presence, and is yours endlessly.

My Saudade

My Saudade

Beloved,

You are my Saudade, that vague and constant desire for something that does not and probably cannot exist...

You are my pleasure that I suffer, my sickness that I enjoy.

A deliciously sweet sickness embedded in the core of my being that smells of ecstasy distraction and devotion.

You are water to the budding flowing of a deep and maddening intimacy that has begun to grow.

You are my "Sensucht" that intense longing that grows deep within my soul.

You are my Solider of Love and I desperately await your home coming, for it's the waiting that is most painful.

You are my hero, my exalted mercenary, my defender of every emotion – I wear your last kiss upon my forehead as a brand. That nausea of emptiness comes over me like a wave of sea-sickness, that painful let down after a glorious high, a growing need after our lips have departed one another.

You are my everything, my confessor and protector, my ever-evolving intensity. You are mine and I am yours.

What I Know

What I Know

Beloved,

What I know But They Didn't ....

I know how painfully cold an empty bed can be at night.

I know the empty feeling of eating alone night after night.

I know the deafening silence of not having someone to talk to.

I know the awkwardness of being that "1" extra on everyone's guest list.

I know the sadness of lonely New Year's Eve nights and praying the next won't be the same.

I know the fear of being unprotected and not being able to sleep at night.

I know the dull flavor of success without having someone to share it with.

I know the numbness of wanting to be touched.

I know the ache of wanting to give, love and care for someone who values your service.

I know what life "IS" without him and I will give everything to never be without him again.

The Wonder of You

The Wonder of You

Beloved,

As I lay here without you next to me in the quiet and the still of the night, I opened the window hoping to feel the midnight air against my skin.

The caress of the warm summer breeze just as I felt the warmth of your touch down the small my back. I begin to remember the feeling of your touch ... The way each finger dips and circles and glides so effortlessly when we are alone and naked....

Those moments ...those energy filled fleeting moments of time with you ...I am desperate for an answer ...to know and understand what it is between you and me. Is it the reconnection of soulmates? Or simply my energy seeking yours? It is a miracle to me .as big as any man-made wonder in my eyes...

I turn to read ...to shake the thoughts of you from my head, but you have become my existence ...I find you in every verse and line...

A sign from the Divine. How such mercy and love exist between us ...and no one is more beloved to me than you ...a wonder to behold as I had no knowledge of your presence until the universe delivered me unto you ...this is the wonder of love ...the wonder of you.

Sefa Noir-Dark Pleasure

Sefa Noir-Dark Pleasure

Beloved,

What is not known about me but may have been suspected, is that I have been broken, damaged, and wounded at my very core. As it began, I was living my life according to the expectations of others. When we met, I was that wounded child -trying to find love the in recognition of my accomplishments.

My self-esteem was non-existent - my inner being consisted solely of efforts made to get others to recognize the person I was. I tried repeatedly to gain strength of character to build on my determination, to be more than the "good daughter" but to find the courage to look and be who I was on in the inside.

He walked into my life and opened the flood gates... allowing me to pour out all the insecurities, fears, tears, and emotions. I showed him the emotional scars and he held it all in his hands and healed it. He healed in a way that I could never have suspected...his discipline and dominance of me daily and continually gave me stability... certainty. an unusual sense of security.

My friends questioned me consistently as to why I would allow a man to subjugate me in this way. I followed his rules implicitly without question, wore his mark under my clothes, and in public among others, I proudly wore his ring. Then it began to happen - in the everyday submission to him I found my sexuality and myself - I found myself able to let go - to just close my eyes and experience the moments that he created for me to experience. I found that I could feel things at a level that I had not known before - I was more than a possession - I had become his connection to his masculinity, and his true sense of self, as he was mine to my femininity. He allowed me to be weak, and I allowed him to be strong. It was protected. It was our world and it was everything to me ----I had become exposed. Our ultimate separation wasn't just the passing of a relationship - he was my protector, my guardian, my friend, my disciplinarian - he was the vessel into which I poured my soul - and he had left with it never to return. He left me open and raw to the world...

I then embarked on the journey of trying to continue to find and define myself without his protection. It was then I first began to embrace spirituality - and seeking to expand my conscientiousness - In doing so I found that I could be extremely empathetic - I could feel the energy of others and be a source of strength to someone, if not for myself ----and so I chose the path of being in the business of people "human resources"... as the moments when I could interview and connect with other spirits became my way of protecting myself, learning and listening in an attempt to avoid being hurt. I had become a student of the human condition- yet I was still naked and raw to the world.

What meeting you has done for me is remind me that my openness to the world needs a protector... a guardian... a watchman in the night. If you allow my openness to find refuge within your protection - then I can hold as many of your cares as you need me to (no limitation).

Grab onto me tightly and demand that I and my love, and my energy are yours alone, and you will find within that demand it will only multiply and expand for you. Hold my hand and wipe my tears and you find they will grow flowers in your garden. Possess my body, mark it yours, and you will know no limitation with it (I'll forever be your pleasure). Look at me, and value my spirit as currency to the universe, and you will know no spiritual lack of your own. Love me as the most delicate thing you have ever held - and my love for you will never break, bend or waiver. Own me in my completeness, and I will be yours now and forever...

Lost

Lost

Beloved,

I am lost. Will you find me?

Will you seek me out on the cold dark days...?

Will you meet me in the quiet and the stillness of the night with nothing to guide us but the moonlight?

I am lost. Will you find me?

Will you join me in the journey of a soul to return to its origin, to elevate to higher ground, will you lift me?

Will you inspire me?

That Day

That Day

Beloved,

That day has finally arrived when nothing else matters except your touch upon my flesh. For each time, we are together deep within the silence of our sexuality, your dark power draws out my vulnerability, my fragility, my femininity and casts aside the veil hiding my personal truth like a page being torn from a book.

Within that instant that you begin to touch me, my soul and spirit exhale the deepest of exhausted sighs and the frigid ice of my composure melts. I transform into a freed prisoner. The euphoria of each Sensation builds, and my addiction to your darkness grows.

That day has finally arrived that our brief interludes of your succulent rawness no longer satisfies me. I am increasingly desperate for you like heroin, I crave that next high.

That day has finally arrived that you have released all my inner demons and they bow to you my Master, the key holder to the prison of My everyday existence. I thirst for you like a desert nomad seeking an oasis —I am replenished and alive when you grab hold.

That day has finally arrived that I beg for your touch as only then am I real, am I alive am I myself. And I am yours.

The Completion

The Attraction

The Attraction

Beloved,

Your attraction is more than the sum of your position, the size of your delicious member, and what you can potentially offer a woman. Your attraction is the unique combination of your entire being and its ability to draw me in, to seek you, to want you. It is your indescribable electricity that passes through my fingertips as I touch your skin, and how your muscles react and release as I massage you - your flesh connects with my feminine sensibilities in just that moment. When my touch can relieve the strain in your neck and lower back and I hear that subtle moan and your deep exhale I feel connected, important and useful. When my lips begin to touch the back of your neck and inhale the mixture of your cologne and dominance - I want to lose myself within you, within the act of pleasuring you.

Your attraction is the refined masculinity of your being, as I watch you undo your cuff-links and the cut of your jaw against the framework of your shirt and tie, it is deep and rich like the tone of your voice when you are providing direction. Your attraction is deeply sensual and methodical, it is detailed and verbose like the terminology you use to describe your past and present. Your attraction is beyond physical, it resides in the intangible ... in your walk, the bend of your fingertip against the back of my hand, and the radiance of your smile from your laughter. Your attraction is much greater than your physical being - your attraction is all that is you.

All That I am

All That I am

Beloved,

All that I am, Mind, Body and Soul belongs to him. I give myself freely and willingly. Not out of fear, but out of love;

My mind is his, to expand, to explore, to know as only He can. I have no secrets from Him, for secrets are a thing that would keep me from being more perfectly his.

My body is his, and if He says I am beautiful, then I am.

My soul is his, as bare to his will as my skin is to his touch. I can always feel his presence around me and inside me; and although we may be many miles apart, I know that He is always with me. I am His and his alone.

This is my promise of devotion.

His

His Beloved,

Women want the title of "his wife" without doing the job that is required to be "his wife". How can anyone expect to be given the "honor" without the "service"? Kings, Queens, Presidents .... etc. ...to gain much, you must give much.

I lie here in bed, quiet and still, and if I close my eyes, I can picture myself lying there next to him ...there is a thrill, a security, a quiet comfort that is easy and familiar when I am lying there next to him. I feel safe in my raw nakedness with him ...he has given me permission to uncover myself both in the flesh and spirit.

There is a joy that comes with my flesh touching his in the middle of the night ...I know he thinks I am just his little "Sex Kitten" that can't get enough of him. And he's right ...I can't ...but it's not just the beautiful orgasm he taught me, or the warm full sensation when he enters that I can't get enough of ....

When I press myself against him in the night and I hear him stir, and he wraps his leg within mine and he moans gently in my ear ...as I begin to feel his need grow against my back ...in this moment, just then I feel closest to him...connected and important. As if I am the only person who can fulfill him or satisfy him at that very moment. I would gladly "serve" him 100 times a day if necessary.... because he needed me.

Why do women run from serving a man? I want to run to it. Run to serving him.

I need to feel him again.

If he Knew

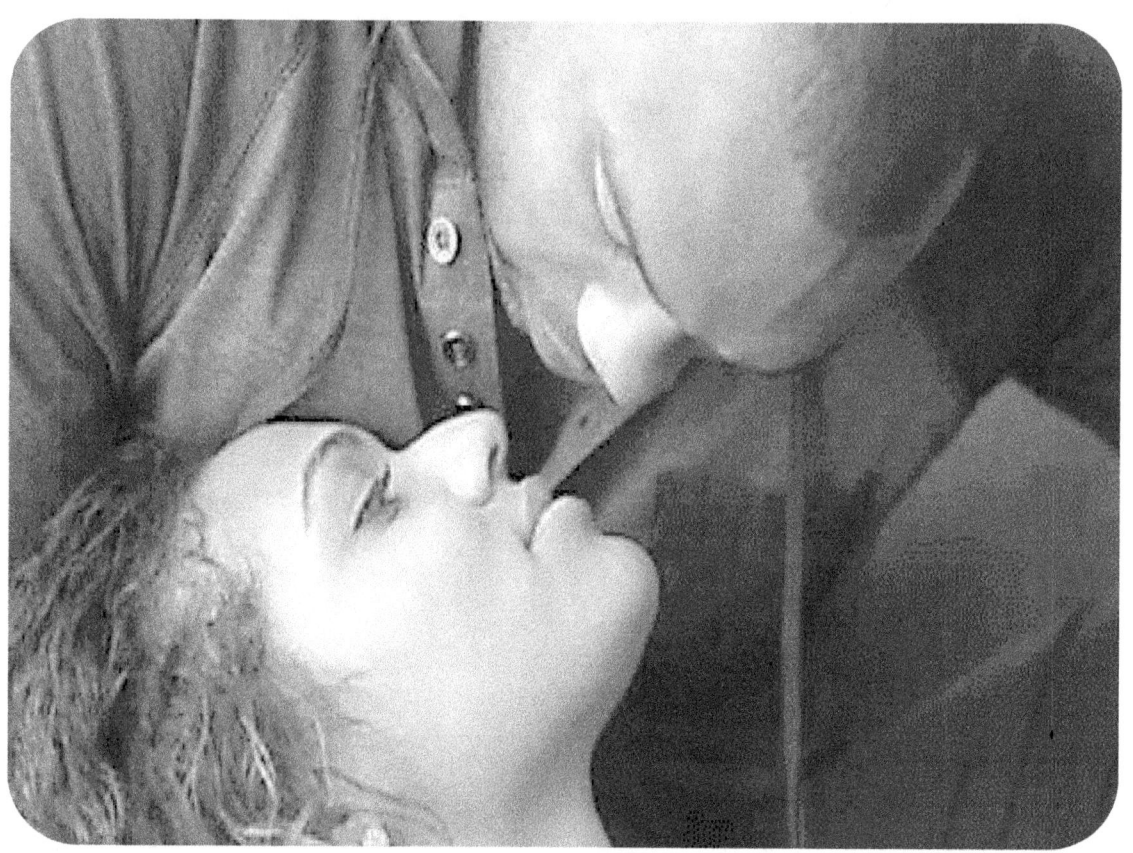

If he knew

Beloved,

If he only knew ......

How afraid I am that no-one will ever truly "love me" ever again.

That every love song I listen to reminds me of him.

That I go grocery shopping at midnight just to keep busy and not think of him.

How many text messages to him I have written but never sent.

How jealous I am of the women that have been able to call him husband or boyfriend.

That I'm not like all the rest.

How happy I was to wake up in the middle of the night and feel his arm around me.

That I would never take him or his love for granted.

That I wanted to just die inside when it seemed as if he thought I was fat.

How scared I was the first time we met, as after he kissed me, I knew I could fall for him. That I need for him to need me.

That I am always thinking of how to please him.

How in love with him I am.

How his intelligence impresses me.

That touching his chest turns me on and makes me feel safe at the same time.

How much he is wanted in my life.

How I crave his ownership.

When he says, "you're mine" means everything to me.

That I adore sitting at his feet. That he is in possession of all of me.

I Want to Love You

I Want to Love You

Beloved,

I want to love you ... I want to love you in a way that makes the ache go away.

That quiets the hunger deep within your chest. I want to love you in a way to mend all your broken pieces and makes you whole again...so I can kiss and caress each beautiful scar.

I want to love you in a way, that my touch heals you, and warms your soul. (it was left out in the cold far too long) I want to love you in a way that what you "do" no longer matters... that you feel loved for just "being".

I want to love you in a way that you see and feel my love for you each day... I want to love you in a way that they write books, and movies about. I want to love you in a way that your flesh cries out for mine in the night ... I want to love you in a way that someday you might love me.

The Soles of My Feet

The Soles of My Feet

Beloved,

And your name was written across the soles of my feet...a symbol of my enslavement to you. As you are with me every waking moment of the day

I say nothing ... yet with each step I take, my body cries out your name. How did I get here? Lost. In a sea of emotions ... desperate for the captor of my soul.

I trace each letter like the blind read braille - yet it is merely paint...somehow you have penetrated me...

I can feel each letter ever so softly, as if to caress your tender form ... needing you.

I touch my feet in the hopes that you shall also feel the warmth of me ....

This simple black ink against my skin.

Again

Again

Beloved,

I long for that connection again...

To feel complete and sacred again,

To be feminine and beautiful again under the fingertips of your touch.

In your presence, I gain a sense of self, purpose and direction.

I am his, and I am free to be me.

I close my eyes and imagine days spent with you in bed ...wanting and waiting for each touch.

To know that his use of me completes him as he pours himself into my flesh.

I dream of a relationship of complete and total consumption-to be all his at every moment of every day.

I tingle at the thought that my presence may please him, I crave his desire of me and will do whatever it takes to make his need of me insatiable...because my need for him is endless.

Together we are secure and tranquil.

My spirit is calmed by his voice and soothed by his touch.

With him I am alive, loved, feminine, safe and whole once again.

I am Bound

I am Bound

Beloved,

Tonight, I climbed in this bed, I leaned my head on this pillow and closed my eyes, yet I could not sleep. There is no warmth here among these sheets because you are apart from me, there is no comfortable place but within your arms

I long to press my head against your chest, the sound of your heartbeat soothes me ...each time we are apart from one another I lose a piece of myself as you have written your name deep within my heart, and claimed it as your property.

You have made me love you in a way from which I cannot escape. I am bound to you by touch, by the smell of your cologne, the sight of a shirt across the bed, by orgasm, by love.

The Tidal Wave

The Tidal Wave

Beloved,

I am still recovering from your tidal wave...

Your birth under the Aquarian constellation was no mere coincidence, truly you are not a "cup barer", but your name is synonymous with Tsunami, as you called forth a torrent from this flesh. Or shall I call you my King Poseidon?... I bow to the sovereignty of your dominance, as you commanded the ocean within me, bringing forth an earthquake of emotion, yes you are my Sea God...

I am still recovering from your tidal wave....As the tears had come, they began to flow and refused to stop...I could not catch my breath... I descended to a place of mourning ... a sadness brought on by the ecstasy of you, your touch, your power...I was grieving ... grieving for all the years I had spent without you, the pleasure of you, the taste of you, the touch of you, the scent of you ... the tidal wave of your dominance.

I am still recovering from your tidal wave....I tried to build a dam to keep out your flood, but your rolling wave into my life has grown into a storm of love, lust, desire, need, yearning, submission, devotion ...I have tried to swim ashore, but each time you have pulled me back like a siren into the depths... I am still recovering from your tidal wave....And as I lay there, tired, spent, full of emotion, desperate and tearful ... I couldn't tear myself away ...had you asked me to, I would have given my flesh again, you are an addiction.

I am still recovering from your tidal wave.

Connected

Connected

Beloved,

Words cannot express the depth of what I feel for you, it is not about the sex, you are and being with you is so much more. Every time you touch me, kiss me, fuck me, bite me, hold me, I feel whole, and complete. There was an emptiness within me that I cannot describe...an aching for you, a craving for your passion. Your strength and control are delicious to me, I taste it with every lick of my tongue against your body...I am addicted.

There are moments in this life when you realize you have a deep need, that previously you were not aware it existed...it is this need that turns to thirst and then grows into a hunger. I have a growing hunger for you....

not purely physical as you are not solely a physical being. I lie in my bed, and recognize that no food, nor drink will satisfy because it is an energy, a vibration, a magnetic pull as if I require to be plugged into you to recharge me....it is a small singular moment that before now I couldn't identify. It's that moment when I begin to feel the sweat drip from your chest, and my legs spread apart wider, you push deeper inside, your grip tightens around my thighs.

I can feel the pulse of you, and the tap behind my navel. It's when my back begins to arch and contort, and my breath becomes short.... it is the transfer of your surplus energy into my womb as if you need to dispel it, your core can no longer contain it.

I am your depository for your excess as it fulfills me and draws me closer to you ...in that singular moment we are connected, and I need it more than I ever realized.

The Submission

Air and Earth

Air and Earth

Beloved,

As his air enters her earth, she can breathe freely.

As her earth is firm and steadfast, she keeps his air intact. His air teaches her to fly high, unrestricted and without hesitation. He brings new colors and sides of both love and life to her monotonous existence. While she embraces him, and gives him the sense of security and importance of stability he craves for in his life.

Air and Earth experience the purest form of love and a new style of devotion, where neither is very expressive but their mutual concern for each other is impressive and definite.

Air and Earth create a sexual blend of imagination and reality. He is unpredictable and always changing. He makes love in many ways. He enjoys hours of making love while giving his entire soul. She is stability and believes in the exhibition of visible and satisfying proofs of sexual intimacy. Her love making is carried out as a deliberate act of his fulfillment. He daydreams in sexual fantasy, which makes her curious and long to be a part of his world, they adjust to the other's love making easily as their love exists on an emotional and mental level - they are fulfillment in its highest form.

His air is expansive, unending, a continuous reach for higher ground. Her earth is definite, and calm, cooling and serene. His air blows ever so gently the petals of earth's hair... together they are bonded by their opposition, their nature magnetic, unceasing *and never ending. Her earth becomes the clay to the potter's hands and is continually molded, moment by moment, breeze by breeze, caught up in the torrent of air's windstorm...*

He lays his breath upon her chest and together they move to a conjoined heartbeat...She is his, and he is hers.

King

King

Beloved,

How I so want to believe you heard my desperate plea to the universe for your return into my world. I look lovingly into the abyss, clutching my heart so very tight with breathlessness, just to catch a glimpse of you…

I often hear your voice in the night, as I try to find other distractions to pull me away from thoughts of you.

Your strength beckons me daily …for it is my femininity reaching for your masculinity ---just barely out of my grasp.

I lay myself at the foot of your throne, an offering in completeness of love and singular devotion…never wanting to be parted from your side….My Beloved King.

Know This

Know This

Beloved,

Know this …there are brief moments of silence deep within our everyday conversation, that I feel as though I can hear your unspoken thoughts and you mine….

Know this…. At 2am as your warm chest lay against my back I am not sleeping, but instead counting each of your respirations as if to save them as a memento of our time together.

Know this…when you reach for my hand and caress my fingertips with the side of your thumb, I am secretly praying that the moment never ends.

Know this …when you clutch my throat and kiss my neck, my entire body goes limp, and all tension and stress depart from me. I am free.

Know this … when your bite marks my flesh, I feel most beautiful as you adorn me with your passion.

Know this …with each passing day I fall deeper in love with you.

I want to know you

I want to know you

Beloved,

I want to know you... to know about you. Have knowledge of you, your flesh, your soul.

I want to dive into your consciousness and know your waking mind.

I want to know the center of your thoughts.

I want to have knowledge of the very timing and pace of your heartbeat.

I want to read your skin like braille and understand each line.

I want to translate your breath with every exhale.

I need to know you, the inner you, the real you, the you shown to no other.

I need awareness and recognition of your being and its very core.

I need to know your questioning, your wakening, your rise and fall.

I need to know that our thoughts meet and kiss as deeply as our lips.

I need to know your sexuality without ever having touched.

At every level of your existence I need to know you...and you know me, and I am yours.

Be Free

Be Free

Beloved,

In waiting for that apology that shall never come, you only hold yourself and our future hostage.

Set yourself free.... as truly that release is more about your soul and its anguish then it is the wrong that's been done.

Unlock your bondage...and ascend your throne.... your reign begins when you can leave the past behind and start anew .... your crown, kingdom, and new Queen await.

Ease your mind, expand your spirit, elevate to the highest ground... Not to forgive... and yes maybe to forget...

But certainly, to gain your freedom from their emotional prison. Your sentence is over - the penance complete- and you need only to walk through the door of yesterday into the palace of our tomorrow.

Redeem Me

Redeem Me

Beloved,

Tonight, I felt that hungry lion that dwells deep within your chest, that beast you keep caged behind those seemingly quiet eyes.

He gazed upon my soul as if to consume me ...I gladly placed myself at his feet. His for the taking ...in of his power to fill this empty space.

Soft and sultry you crept in... during the night.

I sit here and wait for your redemption, waiting for the day you finally arrive to collect my soul, like a missing item in the lost and found.

Waiting as if I had 100 years on my hands, and thousands of grains of sands from the hour glass in my pocket like spare change.

I allow the hours to treat me like a POW in a Vietcong prison camp, all in hopes of that day. That moment ...when you walk through the door and finally touch me again.

Imprinted on My Soul

Imprinted on My Soul

Beloved,

Momma always said be careful of what you ask for …I should have headed her warnings. When I petitioned the universe, I never thought such a request would be granted.

Then you appeared. A beautiful combination of all my heart's bits and pieces, and some of my darkness too…how delicious you are. You inspire me in ways you cannot know, simply by quiet truth, and your open understanding.

How I long to lay myself against your warm naked flesh and call you my own…

Maybe you'll allow me to be your Concubine…at least my flesh would know the joy of you …a wish granted, a dream yet unfulfilled.

Your name imprinted upon my soul.

My Scars

My Scars

Beloved,

I felt as if your fingertips could trace my pain as you touched me-somehow, they had found their way into each of my wounds ...pressing against the very soreness of my soul.

As I felt the warmth of your lips against mine ...I wanted to exhale so deeply into the universe, this breath I have been forever holding ...

The weakness of my flesh...the tiredness of my spirit...the anguish within my heart all on display in that short, short moment as your lips found their way to my neck....

I was powerless in an instant...body, mind and spirit desperate to be claimed. I was naked before you without ever having been undressed.

All my emotional bruises showing like a warrior's battle scars .... but needing to be kissed one by one ... again and again...until they fade.

His Secret

His Secret

Beloved,

Have you not seen that I am a mixture of those...dirty, pretty things? The secrets from inside your jacket pocket that you play with, that no one else dare suspect.

I'm warn and sticky with your fingerprints from all your rubbing when none are looking ...and oh how you just love to watch me lay there naked upon your chest late into the night...

His dirty little secret...an achingly prized possession...a captive of his desire, yet chained to this every day existence and constantly craving to be led by him, to be felt by him ...to be needed by him...above all else just to be HIS.

The Recognition

The Letter

The Letter

My dear brothers, I know it is disheartening when you encounter that angry black woman, that is mistrustful and appears so jaded to the world, when you are only looking for love and comfort of a good woman. Please stop and take a moment on that first date and really look at who you are seeing... What sits across the table is the woman who watched as our men were taken away in chains. She's the woman that worked the fields and raised your children when you were sold away to another owner. She's the woman that watched you leave and fight for our freedom to never return. She's the woman that hid the children and held a gun in the night as you taught her to do so, in fear of the riders that came in the night.

She's the woman that marched alongside you, refused to sit in the back of the bus, and faced the dogs with you. She's the woman that watched you leave for Vietnam and fight for things we didn't understand. She's the woman that brings the children to the prison, so they don't forget Daddy, makes ends meet with not much, and cried as she watched them kill her son in the streets of Compton and Ferguson. Yes, she's angry my brothers...angry because of the struggle she's had to endure, and angry over the loss of you.

Angry for every time she was told her black wasn't beautiful ...to cover her hair, to be the beast of your burden ...but not allowed to shed the tears on your shoulder.

She is your mother, sister, friend ...the nanny ...the favored cook and servant that holds her jaw tight, her head high and too often swallows her pride to keep the children alive... She works tirelessly, puts your dreams before her own, loves deeply and moves mountains as only a Queen does....

My dear sisters... I know that pain in your spirit. That deep, sharp, cutting, pain, that drives and fuels your righteous indignation ... how briefly you want so much to give the man sitting across from you all your heart, but cannot because of that pain. As you reaffirm your conviction when he walks to your door, know who is really standing beside you. He's the man that had to bear witness to your abuse at the hands of a slave owner. He's the man that had to endure watching you cry and hold his son, as they carried him away in chains. He's the man that had to try and affix the memory of your beauty in his mind, as he ran for your freedom.

He's the man that gladly placed his neck in the hangman's noose -rather than have a rider in the night touch a hair on your head. He's the man that walked the streets day in and out after serving uncle Sam and all he got was a heroin addiction instead of a job. He's the man that's willing to accept your child as his own and start anew with you.

He's your brother, your father, and friend - that nice guy next door you've chosen to ignore, that only wants to see you smile. He's the warrior that leads the fight, he's the artifact that was stolen alongside you, he's the King that wants to love you.

Your Queen

Your Queen

Beloved,

You asked me to be your Queen and fight alongside you in the war. You said that your people needed my strength, my power...but most of all my grace.

Then you abandoned your Kingdom and me. You were gone.

Off in the night chasing the riches, the life of a spy, traitor and turncoat could provide.

I honored my promise and stood tall by your people...brought everyone and everything I possessed to your fight...to defeat this virus that you had somehow left behind.

The finally came and We began to build a new, although our realm still seemed empty without you. Yes, I became the leader you predicted I could and would be...but oh the costly price I paid for this crown you bestowed. I sit upon your throne Knowing Though queen I have become ...I have lost the woman inside.

Then you became a King... crowned somehow in this mixed up place of sovereignty....

That crown pushed down so tightly around your noble brow, your pulse quickens with each heartbeat.

I don't envy your reign King, in this awkward realm you've inherited.... Each man alive is an assassin out after your throne.

They are threatened by your mere existence... what it is that scares them so about you, my King?

Is it the broadness of your back, and your ability to carry the weight of your family's cares on your shoulders?

Is it the fullness of your lips and how gentle they can caress?

Is it the might of our fists when you must protect your own...?

Or is it the expanse of your mind... always creating beauty in this ugly world.

Or is it simply the depth and breadth, of the love in your heart.as every Nubian King before you have.... adopting, assimilating, and accepting many that are not their own and woven them in their tapestry?

Pursued by a few, hunted by many. but needed by me most of all...

Waiting

Waiting

Beloved,

These years without you have taught me that I can't find life in dead things. And to live is to taste the sweetness of life's dessert as it drips from your lips.

I crowned you my King even if I were no longer your Queen. I volunteer my enslavement because without your passion, there is no freedom, there is no life.

Life only exists in the fire ...and the fire exists within you ...and with or without you my soul separated from yours continues to burn.

I have died everyday waiting for you.

It's been a slow death, bit by bit.

Losing little pieces of me that I fear I can never get back...

It's been a death that took a thousand years, and the heat of a scorching sun.

Waiting and wanting like a traveler in the desert...

Needy and desperate wanting to breathe you as the air, and drink you as water.

All the while hoping for arrival...

I have died everyday waiting for you.

A Petition

A Petition

Beloved,

I have ascended and risen into this place.... a rebirth as it were into this existence.

All the while never truly leaving my passions behind me.

Wanting and needing to find you....

I have reincarnated myself oh so many times, with the hope that in each life time I might find you beloved...

but you were lost to me... or was it that I was lost to myself and therefore blind to your existence?

I petition the universe with an offering of my energy ...Nightly Novenas for just one moment... just one glimpse...just one touch

I heard your voice in the distance and knew my place was between your thighs.... my surrender.

What transgression from a previous life am I now paying the price - that we are separated.... I need you my soul....

My Love is Dying

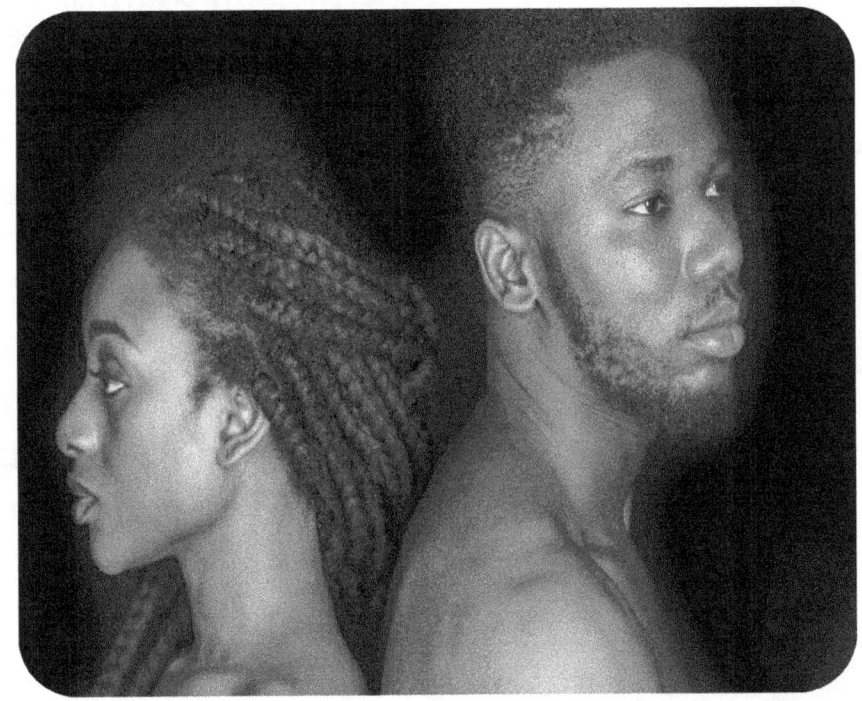

My Love is Dying

Beloved,

My love for you is dying ... like a withering rose upon a sunny window sill in June.

Confused, it struggles and gasps to breathe, desperate to find the light at the end of the tunnel of your absence...

Your fading passion, emotion, gentle kisses and soft words.

My love for you is dying... the slowest of painful deaths, lingering amid the abstract realm of days and hours... waiting and wanting, hoping for the white knight rescue of that one simple sentence. A solitary line from deep within your soul, an expression of you to me.

My love for you is dying...growing more frigid daily just as the air chills when fall nights lengthen, needing the warmth of your affection alongside to defeat the chill that loneliness leaves behind.

My love for you is dying. shall I call 911? Beg for its resuscitation and that you breathe life into it again? Or shall I let it wander, bit by bit, amongst the sunset of tomorrow never to return.

For Love

For Love

Beloved,

I have done many of stupid things in my life as well, and often I have done so for love. I was willing and able to do them even if the result was painful. I did it gladly and openly, and wholeheartedly because it was for love. And even so, after it was rejected or turned away because of what I had done for love - broken and bare to the world, I was not angry.

I wasn't angry because I believed and still do very much believe that loving someone is the greatest thing I could do. It was the one true gift I could give of myself that had value-even if it wasn't valued by that person. My only care became how often or how much of this gift could I give-the well is not endless. And here today I stand before you with all that is left before the well runs completely dry... it is my last...

It's all that remains of a heart that was once so full and strong - and although weaker and almost empty. What remains is the best - the strongest and most resilient of my love -because it has had the courage to stick around waiting for your arrival. So here it is my beloved, that last of a vintage... a collector's edition - and I gracefully offer it to you.

Possession

Possession

Beloved,

I dream of your possession nightly... a slave to your sexuality.

I crave your strength and for the weakness of my flesh to submit to it.

To lay myself naked and bare at your feet, only to be used at your will, with no opportunities for objection.

Lead me in your darkness... those small tight spaces of your mind, and where sex and ownership collide... I need to feel and see the red marks of your teeth against my flesh... consume me as if fresh blood to a vampire.

My inner core tingles at the sounds of your words in my ear... directing me, telling me, ordering, that I can only do your bidding... I long to hear over and over that I am your possession - how the words "I own you" thrill my senses.

I am a woman that desires only what her man desires. To be his every mortal need.

20 Years

20 Years

Beloved,

I love you, I never stopped loving you. All I have ever done is try to replace you. I am not saying this to ask you to take me back.

I just want to stop my heart from filling up all the time.

I know you are happy, and have moved on, and I am ok with that.

I just need to find a way to move on from "us" somehow...

its maddening... I have dated and married, and all were disasters.

I guess I just needed to tell you that you were important to me....

You were my everything.... and I love you and hate you at the same time.

I love you because of who you are, and who we were, but I hate you as well for leaving me (even if it was my fault).

You have ruined me for all others and that's not fair... I just want you to give me my heart back, so I can stop this endless love sickness over you...

20 years is more than enough justice for however I hurt you... I am enslaved to you in a way I just can't explain...

Lifetime

Lifetime

Beloved,

Your fingertips against my skin sing a song of a thousand lifetimes...

I feel your history in every touch.

Your lips pressed tightly against mine speak an ancient language to my soul...

When we are together, I am transported to another lifetime....

I lay across your feet. My body presented as a gift...

You are my Pharaoh. I am your Egyptian Queen....

I feel your closeness... and I drink in the heat of your flesh.

We are the Harlem Renaissance...and the tingling of my body plays your music.

I ache to feel you enter me...throbbing and beating like the drums we left behind in our motherland....

You are my royalty and I your concubine...my flesh serves no other...

Replenish Me

Replenish Me

Beloved,

I have lost and found, seek and have been sought in this life, often wondering my place on this color-filled bauble of existence. I have questioned my reality and endured the pains of lost quests, and loves and my heart has held momentary glimpses of happiness...forever seeking joy in the sunset.

I have looked for my own self determination and stood singularly in my existence. Standing tall and strong, all the while wearing an illusion while no one... only unto myself knowing the endless turmoil in my heart,

How then would I herald your arrival - how would I celebrate your presence? I was empty....

soul and spirit. I have felt that all that was within me had been previously lost and buried ... I traded it ... gave away my essence... sold my being to those often less deserving - I was searching for that joy.

Weak, worn, and wary... and at the end of the journey - like a desert nomad searching for water... you came into my view. I felt warm, and fuzzy... cloudy. my vision needing adjusting... I needed to be clear. I needed to be clear on my discovery as if it was true. if I had found you ...Joy sweet Joy...

And just then, with the gentlest of touches, you replenished me....

His Kingdom

His Kingdom

Beloved,

I want to live in your kingdom.

A subject of your desire.

A citizen of your will.

A Patriot of all your passions.

Knight me a zealot for all your conquests including my soul.

I am your most impassioned emissary - a representative of your quiet darkness!

All who look upon me see only your countenance and good will.

Never knowing that I am enslaved to your Erotica.

Chained and bound by your touch...

Never desiring my freedom...

Existence without my Master, owner, subjugator, leaves me homeless and empty within my soul.

I am his.

ABOUT THE AUTHOR

Sefa Noir's corporate life is a focused executive HR professional, who mentors' employees on careers and their dreams.

When not working as an executive, she writes poetry to record her thoughts, feelings, beliefs and dreams about the human condition, relationships, and love.

To learn more about Sefa Noir and her upcoming soulful works of poetry, visit her profile on The publishing website:

www.AJBPublishing.com or follow her on Instagram @Sefa_Noir

www.ingramcontent.com/pod-product-compliance
Lightning Source LLC
Chambersburg PA
CBHW080443110426
42743CB00016B/3263